Pretty Thoughts

CINDY CHERIE

For all the broken hearts.
I hope these words find you.

I was born with my heart in my mind
and I don't know any other way of surviving it
other than to take all this pain
and make it look pretty.

~ *Pretty Thoughts*

Contents

CHAPTER 1: HEART-SHAPED SECRETS - 8

CHAPTER 2: WITHIN A WEEPING MEADOW - 66

CHAPTER 3: VELVET BULLETS - 117

CHAPTER 1

Heart-shaped Secrets

Blessing or Curse?

Is it a blessing or a curse to feel this deeply? I'm yet to clutch at one conclusion. There are moments of rhapsody I'd sell my soul to live in forever. Split seconds when time decelerates and my eyes close *s l o w l y*. I wasn't sure which of my senses I was a slave to the most in that moment. All I knew was he undeniably appealed to all five. His lips brushed mine and four words seared themselves to the back of my mind- *you taste like equanimity.*

To awaken the love of a poet is to expose them to your elements.

"I know what it is about you," he announced softly brushing loose strands of hair from my face. Electricity spread across my cheek forcing my eyes to flutter shut "…You're pure."

I sighed loudly. "Do you know how it feels?" My voice, barely a whisper in an effort to remain in that space between breaths. The only place I was free from inhaling the perfect chemistry of his cologne dancing with my pheromones. "Do you know what it feels like to be so susceptible to a someone you feel their hands before they touch you?"

He opened his mouth to speak only to hesitate. His brows furrowed, punctuating the silence. *No one plans to end up here,* I thought. It had been two years. Two years of being an invisible character in his life. Two years of waiting on him to love me anywhere other than behind closed doors. I'd lost so much of myself in the process I wasn't even sure I still existed.

It's intoxicating." I resigned, "What chance do I stand against this?" His silence always spoke louder than his words. I was forever begging the screaming to be quiet.

"Can you feel that?" I said, pressing my palm to his chest. "Can you feel how much I love you?"

"Yes," he resigned, hanging his head. "I…I don't deserve it."

That is the curse right there. The eternal torment. Sentenced to mortality feeling people in ways they will never feel you. Hearing their unspoken truth. A life of loving men in ways they will never love you.

Is it a blessing or a curse to feel this deeply?

I know the answer. I've just no desire to abide with both.

Words are my language of love.
Softness has made a home in my throat
causing my mouth to spill heart-shaped secrets.

I promised myself
I would not tell them to another
who did not kiss me like Sunday mornings

I find it hard to speak around him.
Like I'm learning to speak a second language.

I don't know what silences me more-
suppressing my native tongue?
Or my love for him?

We were young at heart
but old in grief
finding one another
bearing bellyfuls of betrayal.
We barely knew each other
but you could have choked on
the air between us-
thick with possibility.

He reached over
and touched my knee
as we drove down the 405
and suddenly
everything smelt like summer
and that was all it took.

-     *To Fall in Love With Him*

I left my heart in San Clemente

Does he sense me
falling against my will?

Every extra second
he breathes love into me?

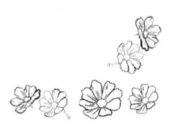

I think you're foolish to play it safe for therein lies the absence of love. I will have nothing of it. I only know of love that consumes me. That even on my best days renders me speechless, pooling around my ankles like liquid strength draining from my bones at the sound of your voice.

Spare me the small talk, I want to know all the ways you've loved and how it broke you. How you laid your heart on the line and they took a sledgehammer to it. I need to know I'm not the only one who spends her days mending what others split. That at a table full of poker faces you're brave enough to feel. I want to see the blood on your hands of lovers lost. The stitches in your side from what they took. I want to hold your flaws in the palm of my hands and love you more because of them.

Are you real like me? Damaged but worthy? Do you love with arms outstretched? Would you jump against all odds? Will you lay down your sword and bare white-flagged-skin? I need to know you're human, guided by the same compass that lead me to you. I need you to know it points in no other direction. Tell me. **Are you brave enough to love me?**

My eyes melt into
swirling pools of rose petals,
delicate for him in ways
I wish I were harder.

He smiles and I blink adoringly-
eyelashes taking pictures.

Oh, how exquisite the agony
of being drenched in love
by the mere sight of someone
and not being able to give it away.

And so it seems
with morning
arrives the flutter
of you.
I awake to the trill
of songbirds
beating in my chest
singing out for you.

Love Is Spoken Here

I don't believe in love at first sight. Something of divine nature couldn't possibly be born of such fickle circumstance. Does time really think it plays a defining role in the acquisition of love? It merely provides opportunities for it to deepen. Before two humans collide there is a predisposition to love that's ignited when souls are compatible. Whether you acknowledge it or not it's there demanding to be felt.

I've never been one to assume the definitive but I believe in moments~ in pockets of time. Love has the most blissful way of drowning reality~ of pushing sensibility beneath the surface till it stops fighting for air and all that remains of it is white noise and the sound of your voice, washing over me like gravel and honey, stripping away years of uncertainty, polishing and refining, calming the warrior within.

And not all love asks to be claimed~ to be labelled as my own. You came as a gentle breeze, brushing against my skin, curious and free of expectations. I was not yours and you were not mine~ just two souls dancing in time. And as I lay here falling asleep to the melody of you I smile upon the simplicity that not all love is deemed eternal.

But for a moment~ this moment~ I'm with you, and you're with me, and love is spoken here.

It was then I knew,
pressed beneath your fire,
lost in skin
that close
would never be close enough.

What is it about the face of love?
I used to want to be
a thousand different things.
Now all I'll ever want to be is yours.

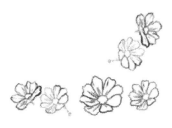

Stories weigh heavy in his eyes
cinnamon tales of cities I've never been.
Fragments of moments I cease to exist.

It's curious is it not?
The pull of human connection?

Part of me knows he'll never be mine.
The other wants to go back in time
and lay alongside him
in all the places he ever felt lonely.

When I say I need you
to love me like the birds
I mean with open hands.
I mean, *be still.*
I mean if you let me
build a home in you
I will always come back.

When they ask me
how many stories are left in me
I will tell them

as numbered as the days love takes to find me
and an eternity more spent writing you.

I think of all the men I've loved.
The men whose hands drew
constellations across the universe of my skin.

I think of lovers long gone.
Men who left me
to connect the stars
and find my way back home.

I'm still finding my way.

I think of being loved
and when I think of being loved
I always think of you.

Your fingertips have never traced my outline
but when you say my name
the firmaments in your eyes fade to blue,
each syllable dripping with sweet revere
and I am safe in the eye of the storm.

And I need you to know
that you're a hurricane
that falls for me like summer rain
and it's the closest thing
I've ever felt to being loved.

– *Storm Boy*

I'm not always this quiet around people but there's this air of nonchalance about you.

Has anyone ever told you every time you smile the sky falls gently?

I try to appear unaffected by such things. Like that day your laughter lent humanity to the ocean air and I climbed atop your lap, covering you in sand. The sun knew what I was thinking. It hid behind the clouds as I kissed your neck, swallowing my thoughts, filing them away under things I'll never tell you-

I want you,
> *I want you,*
>> *I want you.*

"I'm sorry. I'm rambling again." You laugh apologetically. "I should go to bed."

"No." I smile into the phone. "You're not."

I wish I could say more but vulnerability severed ties with me long ago. I keep sending her flowers but she never replies.

Someone whose heart does not resemble the ruins of Notre Dame might confess why I fall like a house of cards every time you tell me stories. They would say the human voice is the purest of all instruments. That the base in your voice lulls me. That you make me wonder if something that precious could ever be restored to its former glory?

I say *Goodnight* and hang up the phone but what I mean is, if distance was not a thing I would crawl into your bed and press my ear to your chest. I mean I've forgotten what a warm body feels like. I mean you sound a lot like what it feels like to remember.

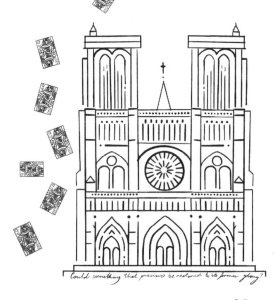

Could something that precious be restored to its former glory?

Can you hear it?

Every time you smile
my eyes scream your name.

I'm lost in the eyes of men and when I say lost I mean, I won't be found. People say love will find me but heartbreak left me somewhere amidst the treetops and wounded birds forget how to fly and when I say forget I mean, refuse to remember.

It was seven o'clock on a Tuesday morning when perfection came along and stole the air clean from my lungs and when I say perfection I mean, I forgot I had knees.

He wore Clark Kent glasses and a James Dean smile and for the first time in years I remembered falling felt a lot like flying and when I say falling I mean the four-letter-kind- and suddenly I noticed how high I was and when I say high I mean lost in his eyes and for the first time in years I wanted to be found.

It was 5:32 pm when everything went a little hazy. I remember because I pressed the home button of my phone balancing on my left knee in an attempt to appear unfazed about the way my senses bowed down the second he sat on the park bench alongside me. I've never been good with numbers. I muddle at the sight of them but my ovaries proceeded to count the minutes following his arrival.

I tried to find where I was up to in my book before I lost all collectedness. The words blurred together uncooperatively. I turned the page.

"Do you come here often?" He panted, trying to catch his breath, reaching down to tighten the laces of his runners.

My eyes lingered on an eagle wrapped around his left arm in black ink, glistening beneath a layer of sweat. I bit down on my curiosity, swallowing the urge to ask what his connection to the tattoo was.

"Sometimes," I replied politely, pressing my lips together. "It's peaceful...and the sunset likes to put on a show." I pointed off in the distance to where the edge of the ocean kissed the sky.

"I can see that," he smiled, raking his fingers roughly through the tangled mess of his hair, throwing his head back, emptying the contents of a water bottle over his face. Something behind my ribcage winced instinctively and I swear a concord of angels started singing somewhere in heaven. I cleared my throat and glanced at the time. 5:33.

We sat in unison sharing the absoluteness of silence.

"It's quiet here," he expressed softly after a few minutes. "I can see why you like it." He stared straight ahead, eyes resting pensively on the horizon. A waterfall of truths threatened to fall out my mouth. Resisting, I continued reading my book absentmindedly sifting through his pages.

I checked the time. 5:35.

"Are you expecting a call?" he nodded towards my phone.

"Ah, no," I shook my head, embarrassed. "I'm just keeping track of how long it takes."

"For what?"

"For me to make a fool of myself and tell you you're the most beautiful thing I've seen all day."

You are a kingdom,
strewn with fairytale girls
and foreign sights,
and I am a lone mermaid
allured by the beauty of distant lands.

I have memorized a thousand and one reasons
why castles are no place for a barefoot wanderess.
I wrote each and every conclusion
meticulously upon the bricks of my imagination
and recite them on nights I'm tempted to fall in love
with the way your smile resembles
the Northern Lights from across the sea.

A slave to curiosity I may be,
but naive I am not.

I've read your happily ever after.
It speaks of a girl with much less salt in her skin
than I.

Be that as it may,
it still doesn't stop my sense of wonder
from washing ashore and imagining
what it might feel like to make love to you
beneath a blanket of stars
every time I close my eyes.

BETTER LEFT UNSAID

It must have been around six o'clock. The telltale signs of a day's ending drifted lazily across cotton candy skies. Remnants of perfect moments hung in shades of pink, orange, and blue. When I was a little girl I used to think God would take out a paintbrush and paint the clouds prettier to mark days I must remember. Some part of me still thought it to be true.

"Why are your fingers stained blue?" his forehead creased with concern as he reached for my wrist. The familiar sound of a jet plane engine hummed overhead.

"Look!" I pointed, stuffing my hands quietly into the pockets of my jacket. "Make a wish."

Momentarily distracted he looked up and smiled murmuring something in Spanish I wanted to capture in a mason jar and place on a shelf. His dimples creased and for the briefest of seconds I allowed myself to imagine pressing my lips to the scar on the side of his nose only to tell him he was everything she ever told him he was not.

But when boy's eyes mirror stories of fading sunsets some things are better left unsaid. I was just a girl whose ink-stained fingers had spent too many a night writing letters that would never be sent- and I loved him in ways he'd never know.

We don't talk about braving forward motion.
How we must teeter dangerously
on the edge of vulnerability
to allow others to move us.
He grabbed my hand before crossing the road,
leading me out of a dark place,
and I didn't know how I felt about him
but for the first time in twelve months
I was not swallowed up in loss
and for a moment, that was enough.
That was enough.

I'm never sure of anything.
Not anymore.
I tell myself it's safer this way-
to lay down alongside
the uncertainty of this life
and all of its disappointments.

Who am I to assume the definitive?

But there you were, sweet creature,
looking like everything that's good in this world,
humbly explaining calculus to a girl
with no hope of ever remembering,
tracing symbols in the sand with your finger,
stealing my questions marks,
unaware of one thing.

I could love you.

If I ever allowed.
One day.
In an alternate universe
where hearts are safe
to bet on a sure thing.

The absoluteness was deafening.

I could love you.

$$y = \frac{1}{x}$$

$$x^2 + y^2 = 9$$

$$y = |-2x|$$

$$x = -3|\sin y|$$

I want him.
Every love-stained piece of him.
I want to trail kisses down the valley of his chest,
inhale the chemistry of his skin,
run my fingers through his hair and bite his bottom lip,
smile into his mouth and wrap my arms around his neck.
I want to read him,
drag my nails softly down the stories of his spine,
giggle when he shivers.
I want to forget the world exists,
explore the maze of his eyes,
whisper his name when I'm lost,
brush my lips against his neck,
feel my chest beneath his chest,
grip onto the back of his shoulders,
make love till my body screams
stop
and then when I'm done,

I want to do it all again.

I know he thinks I'm all boarded windows and Fort Knox
but I do not build walls to keep men out
rather hold tsunamis in.
I drown men like him- men who make paintings out of
women.
Picasso said there are only two kinds of women,
goddesses and doormats,
and I can't help but wonder
which one loving him would surely paint me to be.

I'm no fool.

Oceans have further to fall
and the acoustics of him alone quickens a fire in my skin.
He does this thing where he says my name,
all tongue and cheek in a foreign accent,
and I try to act unaffected by the way it sounds rolling off
his tongue.
Like nectar.

  Dripping.
  Down.
   His.
  Chin.

And I wonder how many lovers
that smile alone has mounted
to the walls of his museum.

I know he thinks I'm all boarded windows
and Fort Knox
but it's the safest place to be.
At least until I work out how
to stop the visions of him picking me up
and pinning me against the nearest wall
from playing *over and over* in my mind.

The way he says "lovely"

as if shamrock
spills out his lips
and onto my hands,
as if the roots of
wild cherry trees
have buried themselves
beneath his voice.

— *Irish Accents*

Mariana Blue

"No one wants the love of a writer." I lamented, stripping the leaves off a nearby branch and tossing them in the air. Autumn crunched beneath my feet. "We take ordinary men and weave them into something remarkable."

"Uh, first of all. Don't take it out on innocent trees and secondly, how is that a bad thing?"

"It just is," I retorted. "Believe me. A writer's heart is no respecter of men, or distance, or possibility. They'll describe you. Each and every part of you, in dreadfully-meticulous detail."

"I think I'd like that."

"I think you're wrong. No man does. At least, not when he looks in the mirror and sees eyes unremarkable. To be seen as anything more is too much of a burden to carry."

"I find that hard to believe," he teased leaning in close to tower over me, hands either side of my shoulders. My back pressed hard to the tree trunk behind me with nowhere to escape, eyes locked on mine, "Go on then, he smiled. "Describe them."

"Describe what?" Maybe there had been a sudden temperature spike in the middle of May or maybe it was because his lips were three inches from mine but my cheeks burned red.

"My eyes, silly," he laughed methodically.

"Ah, no," I objected, attempting to push past him.

"And why not?" He poked fun, grabbing at my waistline, refusing to move aside. "I'm about as ordinary as they come. Prove me wrong. Describe them as something 'remarkable'." He thought himself clever using air quotations for comedic effect.

I might have found it humorous had the answer not been hiding behind my teeth since the first time we met. I knew the repercussions of spilling honesty. It could not be wiped away. My jaw clenched, buying time, afraid of the inevitability that my lips would give way to a crescendo of truths. My chest rose instinctively, holding my breath, only to fall, releasing with it my better judgement.

"Did you know the deepest part of the earth is the Mariana Trench?" The words fell out my mouth as if they had been trapped inside my voice box for far too long. "It's a crescent-shaped trough in the depths of the Pacific Ocean." I peered up at him nervously. I could sense the wheels turning in his mind as he shifted his stance, searching to connect the dots.

"No, I've never heard of it but don't try to change the subject, missy. Describe them."

"Mariana Blue," I replied matter-of-factly. "Your eyes- they're Mariana Blue." Slowly but surely, the silence settled in and I could almost count him connecting the dots, one by one, drawing across his face the expression of a man unable to swallow the love of a writer. "And I'd like to think I'm treading water right now, but you're a little too close."

"S-sorry," he pressed back, releasing my waist. He paced back and forth pensively, lost in thought. "Maybe," he finally said after what felt like an eternity. "It's not that men don't want such a love rather don't know what to do it. I mean, I've seen the way you observe the world. I wouldn't even know how it feels to see with such sincerity."

I thought about the repercussions for a moment and the weight of what I was about to say next. "Two years." I paused, "Two years have passed since I fell into them. It was a Monday. You walked into the room wearing that blue jacket that makes your eyes sound like a siren's song and truth be told I've been drowning ever since."

Somewhere Over the Rainbow

Did you know that light slows down when it enters water? I used to wonder if there was a science to love until that morning you grabbed me by the waist and pressed me against the concrete wall of that carpark. Time decelerated and all seven colors dispersed in an arch across the sky.

Now every time I see a rainbow I wonder who else has fallen impossibly in love.

I know when you look in my eyes you see the Great Barrier Reef and that's too much wonder for any single soul to discover. But if the rain ever stops pouring and you're ready for a love adorned in gold, swim out and find me somewhere over the rainbow.

To love you any less
would be a lie.

It's bittersweet
is it not?
The taste of
falling in love
with someone
you can't keep.

If I'm crazy at all,
I'm crazy about you.
Love is rapping so loudly on my ribcage
and I cannot answer
anything but the phone.

I cross oceans and time zones
to synchronize with you.
I reach
and reach
and come up with fistfuls of the Pacific.

You are the rise and the fall,
the cure and the cause.
In a sea full of possibilities
all I see is you.

Before I hang up I whisper
"I miss you"
and what I mean is
I do not know how to exist in a world
where I cannot kiss your face.

Maybe I am insane
but then you say "I miss you too"
and for a soft sweet second those four words
are the medicine to my madness.

You do this thing
where you belly laugh
and your happiness
is so contagious
it makes my cheeks burn red
and I swear to God
in that moment I forget
every other human exists
but you.

I think of you
and the River Nile
bursts its banks
and floods my thoughts,
coursing from the crown of my head
to the tips of my toes;

and as my knees hit the earth
I ask Hati for just one thing~

to remove this rushing
and place it in your heart
so you might know
how it feels to overflow with love
at the very thought of you.

I feel too much
to ever unfold gracefully.
A slave to my senses,
it all burns straight through me.

Every.
        Elemental.
                Moment.

Ask me of love and
I'll write of wildfire sweeping my skin.

Don't light a match
and ask me to love you slowly.
You already consume me.

Consume me

I am nose-deep
in love with you,
on my tip toes,
head tilted back,
trying to catch
my breath.

"I've never been good at saying things out loud," I confessed.

"There's no need," he replied. "Your eyes speak for you. As if words are an afterthought."

I know you've heard it
a thousand times
but before you go to sleep,
I need you imagine
that I'm not 7000 miles away,
that I'm right there looking up at you,
hands cupping your face,
thumbs stroking your cheeks,
eyes brimming with tears,
the words barely a whisper.
"I love you."

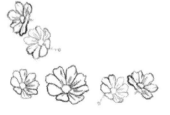

DARK KNIGHT

"There's so much light in you." I say it over and over in the hope that one day you'll see it too.

I sensed it that summer night. Your eyes, smoldering-ebony. Moonbeams filtered in through tiny slits of your bedroom window, as if returning home to your skin, tracing your silhouette and like a shooting star I fell for you.

I have loved you ever since. My raven-haired dark knight.

Did you know when the sun goes down in Chile the Atacama Desert becomes one of the darkest places on earth? The darker the night the more stars visible to the naked eye. I want to go there one day with nothing but a backpack and love in my hand.

I laid on a mountain top once, trying to count the stars. They muddled together like squabbling specks of stardust fighting for my attention. My mind retraced that moment the first time we kissed, as if parallel in feeling, kindred memories threading themselves together through space and time.

I've always thought the firmaments hold a sense of familiarity ~a forgotten nostalgia~ a language we no longer speak. People ask me why I love climbing mountains at dusk and the only answer my heart can string together is up there in the darkness God opens the windows to heaven and when I behold it I feel closer to home.

"I only care for matters of the eternities," I tell you on days I feel the weight of mortality crushing me for there are more stars in the sky than grains of sand on Earth and one day I plan to backpack the world and count them all. The great

astronomers say if we were to stare up from the Andean mountains in Chile elevated upon one the darkest vertices known to mankind the human eye could still only see four and a half thousand stars. But with your hand in mine, Dark Knight, I think I'd see them all.

I will kiss you
with such
tenderness
the mark of my lips
will linger
long after
my departure.

I will stay with you.

I am fluent
in many verbs
yet all I've
been ever able
to do
is love you.

There is gentleness about him.
An unspoken tenderness I can't quite shake.
Words spill from his mouth like summer leaves,
spiralling lazily beneath the trees.

Softly. Safely.

I catch them as he lays lips
upon the bed of my cheek
and I can't help but wonder
if all women's eyes before mine
have closed instinctively
as mine do.

Languidly. Heavily.

Is it just me?

Or has every woman he's ever graced
fallen asleep to the possibility of lifetimes
spent hushed by such meekness,
ear to his chest,
filling the silence with love
in all the quiet places of the world.

Love is no respecter of distance. Neither are words. Seven hundred and forty-two. That's how many times the sun has set across our hemispheres. Seven hundred and forty-two days since you cast a line across the Pacific and caught my eye.

They say a sigh is an expression of longing- a s t r e t c h of the lungs. All I know is my breath faltered that morning you smiled through a pair of Clark Kent glasses and my lungs have been stretching ever since~ whether to reach for or release the impossibility of you. Someone asked me today why I write and the only explanation I could offer was *love and words are the same thing*.

I've never been sure of much. Definitives unravel me but there's one hundred and sixteen thousand libraries on this planet and I hate that I know I could have filled each and every one of them with words for you. What I mean to say is I hope she loves your smile as much as I ache to write about it a thousand different ways.

And I don't think of how it might feel to fall asleep next to you often ~I swear~ only when you look at her like she's an angel plucked straight from the sky and I think to myself *that could have been me*.

Kiss me
like you
kiss her.

I want to know
how love tastes.

I hate the way
my eyes
betray me
when they see you.
The way they say

here I am, love me.

You are my Halley's comet–
a once in a lifetime love.

He doesn't know it but every time he smiles my hands uncurl. I've always been this way- always felt people from afar~ longed to reach out and touch the intangible. Bound by energy I'm drawn towards the music of him. Do you ever close your eyes and listen? I do. He steals my emptiness and replaces it with words.

Honesty has always had the most graceless way of chaining itself to my wrists and my ankles. Forever its slave I've learnt to bite my tongue and swallow my truths~ and by truths I mean the way I want to rip off the way he has muse written all over him and replace it with me~ and by me I mean my hands in his hair. I mean lips painting skin. I mean bodies writing symphonies till we run out of words~ and by words I mean breath.

I know he's out of my reach but his laughter alone fills a bridled soul like mine with the desire to run away with him. He says he's just a boy without the slightest clue how remarkable he really is.

And I wonder if anyone has ever told him? Ever held his face between their hands and whispered the truth~

"You are an infinite adventure."

"Do you love him or do you love loving him?" she asked.

I paused, contemplating the question. My mind simmered on the moment I told you I like things black and white but with you everything is grey.

"Both"

When I think about letting you go I think of that day two years ago I stood beneath the Burj Khalifa in Dubai.

"It's the tallest building in the world," my friend told me as I craned my neck. Its spired tip pierced the sky.

I remember wondering how many man hours it would have taken to build such a monument. Minutes are such finite things disintegrating like crumbling sandcastles victims to an unforgiving tide. We give them away knowing very well we'll never get them back.

My sister is forever telling me I'm possessive. That growing up I never liked giving my belongings away. That I hold things I treasure close to my chest. Time has always been precious to me and yet, I would give you all of mine. That first time you called and we heard each other's voice we started building love whether consciously or not. Every phone call, text, story, laugh, photo, kiss, brush of the skin~our hands were building. I think about how tall we've grown since and the possibilities of our future. What would happen if it all came crashing down? Maybe you would walk away unscathed but the aftermath would surely crush me.

"They're already building another skyscraper taller than this in Saudi Arabia," she said watching me admire the architecture. "Just to knock this one off its throne as the tallest building in the world."

Why do we do this? Why do we dedicate precious hours to building things only to abandon them in the hopes of something greater? Why do we build monuments only to watch them fall? I've never been good at goodbyes. My hands clench into fists as if refusing to let go. I understand that not everything I love is meant to stay but still I hold on, clutching memories close to my chest.

Maybe I don't want to start all over again. Maybe I want to keep building with you. Maybe hearing your voice amounts to the sweetest seconds of my day. Maybe, given a chance this could be the tallest love the world will ever know. Maybe the reason I reach for you is because for the first time in a long time I feel something real and maybe ~just maybe~ my trembling hands reassembling our crumbling ruins is my way of saying, *"Stay. Please don't go."*

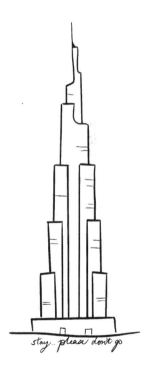

stay... please don't go

Peter Pan

There is magic in the way you carry yourself that makes me
dream of a different life. One where I abandon reality for
the second star to the right. I miss you on nights I don't
hear your voice and leave the window open. To fall for you
would be an awfully big adventure but I've lost myself in
enough Lost Boys to know it never ends well for me in
Neverland.

I ask for love and they hand me a button.

I sigh. You weigh up the heaviness in my breath with
childlike bewilderment and ask me what's wrong. I tell you
I wish I could fly away. You tell me to think happy thoughts
as if that will cure me and I think of you.

If I've learnt anything about this heart of mine it's that it
never stops reaching. I would spend the rest of my days
sewing your shadow back on in the hopes you'll one day
stay, knowing very well you are Peter Pan, and I am
Wendy, and it doesn't matter how many times I leave the
window open you will always fly away.

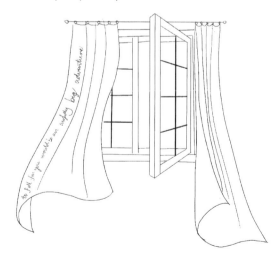

In the summer of 2016 an elderly woman with weathered skin placed her hands either side of my face and stared into my eyes, sifting through a pile of thoughts only the sands of time could have accumulated.

"You have the gift of sight," she smiled. "God filled your eyes with poetry, and that, my dear, is why you feel so much."

I never did get her name just the memory of how soft her hands were imprinted upon my mind.

"It's a curse," I replied. "Some people fill me with so many words I swallow them whole and fall silent."

"Words are not yours to keep."

I remembered that moment as we leant against the pier. You pointed off in the distance, eyes laced with nostalgia, telling me how much you loved swimming and how in yesteryears before the world cut you open you would jump off the edge and swim the mile back to shore. You kissed my forehead and my eyes closed instinctively, heavied by the essence of you.

There was so much I could have said but I am yet to find my voice in a world that continues to misunderstands me. Instead I counted the cracks in the boardwalk as a thousand and one ways I could build a home around you. I placed my hand in your back pocket as if leaving notes there you'd one day find after long forgetting my name.

They would read something like~

I know the hands of time have not held you gently but I've closed my eyes and fallen asleep to sound of kindness beating in your chest night after night. You deserve all that is good in this world. They would tell you how your voice in a darkened room is the sound of reason. That when I pressed my lips to your scar what I meant was~ *you are a miracle.*

I would write of how music plays in your eyes like a distant song that even on my tiptoes I will

never.
        quite.

                reach.

I know our stories have different endings yet, despite it all, I meant what I said~ if in another life we are written on the same page at the same time, in the same colour ink, I will find you and show you what it means to be loved.

CHAPTER 2

Loss

Within a Weeping Meadow

All I ask is that you
be tender with me
while hope crumbles
from my teeth,
while I unlearn the curve
of your laughter,
while I lull this dream
to sleep.

Please, be tender with me
while I lose you.

Broken Clocks

People keep telling me *I have so much time* but I don't know what that means anymore because everywhere I turn are broken clocks~ and for a moment in time you felt like mine but now the hands have stopped moving.

I knew from the moment I asked for a lemon lime bitters and you slid that glass across the table all tongue and cheek and said, *"I don't know if there's any alcohol in it. I told the bartender to surprise me,"* that insubordination was embedded deep within those dimples and for the first time in years I thought I'd found someone worthy to stop checking the time for.

Do you know when I heard the clock start ticking? You tried to push me against the wall and kiss me but you tripped and fell at my front door and I crawled on top of you laughing and I kissed your face *~over and over~* till your cheeks stopped burning red and we forgot why we ever wanted to say goodnight in the first place. For those few fleeting seconds I forgot I had a past or that I ever was broken.

I keep telling myself I will forget the way your hand always found mine crossing city streets or how you made time disappear that night I shivered counting falling stars and you twirled me by an ebony sea and I said, *"You smell really good,"* and I threw myself at you in the stairwell, kissing you for the first time, breathless from the cold, ashamed by my lack of control and said, *"I blame it on your cologne,"* and you smiled and answered, *"I blame it on the stars."* We were in such different places but standing side by side. Remember how I huddled between your legs in the sand dunes and you told me how much you hated the way sand felt sticking to your hands? While I just kept trying to clutch it, watching it slip through the hourglass never knowing if you ever felt the magic of our moments the same way I did.

Like that night I sat on your kitchen counter in a chequer-mini skirt. All you had on was a pair of denim jeans and a smile that made my ovaries hurt. You sliced open an avocado telling me stories all cavalier. Your mouth was moving but all I could hear was *tick-tock* and your back muscles taunting me to reach out and sink my teeth into them. I pulled you in by the hem of your jeans and wrapped my legs around your waist trying to hold time ransom. I never could.

Or how I only wore that red dress on your birthday because I wanted you to take it off and how you carried me to the bed and kissed me till I forgot where your body began and mine ended and you asked, *"Can I make you mine?"* And I held your face and whispered *"Yes."* But what I meant was- *I already am.*

Remember how you taught me to salsa in front of your fireplace and I tripped over your feet because I couldn't think about anything other than the way your hands felt around my waist? I wanted more. I always wanted more. But you never wanted to hear the way my eyes ~in brave moments of vulnerability~ whispered, *"Can I keep you?"*

Now all that's left of us is broken clocks and a handful of sand slipping through my fingers. And if the manacles of time ever start moving again and I unlearn our easy way please know that you moved me in all the ways you never let me confess.

X·VII·MMXXI

Do you know that feeling of standing at the ocean's edge?

The way the waves push and pull against your ankles.
The sense of sinking as sand collapses beneath your feet.
I stood there today
allowing the waves to give and take,
crash into me and then without so much
as an apology leave.

That's how it always was with us.

You, always coming and g o i n g.

Me, forever standing in one place
while the world crumbled at my feet.

\- *Waiting on You*

I was only yours for one winter.
One intoxicating winter.
And despite it all,
despite it all,
it was the warmest winter
I've known.

- *You Felt Like Summer*

Love has this way
of making me stand
on my tiptoes.

Always that little bit
out of reach.

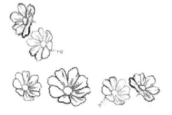

Your silence curls me into
a crescent moon.
Knees to chest, I close
my eyes,
my mouth,
my heart.

I cannot remember the last time
I held thoughts in my hand.
As I pick up a pen and write
it seems everything I've lost comes back to me.
Every word, an arrival.
Poetry collects me like that.
It's raining today.
The sky is bitter and uninviting
as if warning me to go inside.
A grey-somber hum looms overhead.
It's a formidable sadness I find strangely comforting.
I do not covet blue skies on days like today.
Instead I think of all the ways to be invisible,
cloak myself in them, draw a hot bath
and hide from the world.

To be a woman is a colossal thing.

A colossal, t i r e s o m e, thing.

It's not that I am incapable of bearing
the burden, rather,
rainy days have the tenderest way
of reminding me
there's only so much weight a body can carry,
and eventually, we all fall apart.

PTSD

My chest hurts today. I google: *sharp stabbing pain to the left of my sternum* and wonder if you really can die from a broken heart. I pass by a woman in the bitter-cold, my boots sloshing through the muddy wet. She smiles warmly asking me why I walk into work wearing headphones every morning. I say, "I like the way they hug my ears," but the truth is they fill my head with noise that is not born of me. I count of my fingers the number of days I've gone without hearing your voice. I tell myself I've done this before and I can do it again. I write in my journal: **I'm the kind of tired that sleep doesn't cure- tired of losing people I love.** My sister tells me if I stand up straight, and say out loud: **"I'm going to be okay without you,"** eventually I will start to believe it. Today I don't.

Grey is the colour of the sky as I drive an hour up the highway. The windshield keeps fogging over making it impossible to see more than two metres ahead but I'm used to navigating life this way. It's been raining four days straight and I wonder if heavy hearts control the weather. The therapist's eyes, soft and inviting, usher me in. I sink into a blue couch. She asks me what my anxiety feels like and I think to myself~ like being pushed off a cliff without a parachute. She tells me our *subconscious* minds store beliefs we may not know are there and if I can learn something, I can unlearn it too. "When was the first time you recall feeling anxious?" she asks. I remember being sixteen and in a car. A smashed mug. A fractured family portrait. I push it down.

A friend tells me, "You're so beautiful. You'll find someone new." I fake a smile that spells- I'm d o n e t r y i n g.

My feet drag up the two flights of stairs to my bedroom. I hold my phone with both hands, type **I miss you** then hit backspace 8 times. I sit on the edge of my bed, stare into the mirror, forcing the corners of my lips into a crescent moon. The black under my eyes looks like smeared hope. I mouth the words, I'm-going-to-be-okay and ask God to teach me how to uncurl my hands with grace. I fall asleep with my headphones on.

I dream that you hold me and say, "Everything is going to be okay."

I awake to my 5:15 alarm and think back to the last time we spoke. You're on loud speaker and I tell you through tear stained vision, "If you love me you'll come and find me."

I tell myself I won't wait forever
but I worry I will.

Some days I am done with writing.
It is always on the same days I am done with love.

Perhaps the years
will fold in
on themselves
and I will unlearn
our familiar way
but for now, I ache.

Did it feel like rain?
The way I fell for you?
The way you let me
slip through your fingers?

I dreamt last night
you were sitting on a rock
in the middle of river rapid.
I was swimming against the current
to get to you.
I never did get any closer.
The turbulence carried me away.

Don't you ever say I walked away.
You pushed me.

Stowaway Love

I never got to meet your mother and thank her for giving you her eyes. I awoke wanting to tell you that Christmas morning. The sun seeped through my window like auburn molasses reminding me that this morning last year was the first time you told me you loved me. Do you remember? All smitten and split by hemispheres, I called you from the stairwell of my parent's home and wished for distance to fold itself in half, over and over, till I could pull the earth beneath your feet towards my toes.

"I wish you were here," you said.

"Next Christmas," I promised. `

You always told me you couldn't catch a vision of us but that morning dreams reeled in my mind like scenes from one of those nauseating Hallmark holiday movies you would never watch...

It's snowing and we're driving through your hometown. Your hand reaches over the gearstick to find mine the same way it always did- like a ship with no coordinates, anchored to my love. I'm shivering in your jacket and you laugh, shaking your head at the way winter never fails to turn my lips sky blue. I wrinkle my nose and you kiss it adoringly. Your sisters tease you, calling you the Pied Piper for the way you can't

*leave a room without a trail of nieces and nephews trailing behind and
I slip into the kitchen to hug your mother, tell her she can stop worrying
now. I will take care of you.*

I don't know how I'm supposed to feel since we drifted
apart. All I know is Christmas has come and gone for
another year and when the current took you my dreams
became stowaways.

All I ever wanted
was for you
to put down the umbrella
when you said,
"I love you too."

You were a storm chaser
and I, a storm.

It did not matter
how wild I raged
you were *never* going
to let me in.

Unloving you
is like trying to
remain perpetually awake.

I am only human.

Eventually sleep takes me.

I dream of you
and wake up smelling
of loneliness.

This feeling is so deep
I cannot find
an end to it.

I'm unravelling
and not
even
the
floor
can
catch
me.

I do not know
how to describe
this loneliness
other than
I am surrounded
by people
and you are not here.

Let's not pretend we couldn't have been something wonderful. That we did not want for anything more that night your index finger traced the stars and I shivered beneath the blanket of a winter sky. That the firmaments did not behold a million and one reasons I could love you.

Let's not pretend you couldn't possibly see a future by my side. That I took up too much space to ever mold perfectly into yours. That I would not have painted doors upon my every wall if you had but asked and with pacific eyes whispered *come home.*

Let's not pretend I did not buckle beneath your touch. That our nights would not have been spent reading books and making love- burying the past between bedsheets like rolling waves, till our bodies washed ashore like shipwrecks, then rolling waves, then shipwrecked again.

Let's not pretend we did not simply find one another a little too late. That I was not love in its purest form kneeling at your feet. And tell me, is it safe to stop pretending you were not everything I've ever wanted vacantly staring back at me with nothing left to give?

I do love you,
you said,
like dregs of water
rolling around
the bottom of
an empty cup.

I still remember
the tone of your voice,
the shatter of glass,
the words you left unsaid-

just not enough.

I HATE THAT YOU LEFT LIKE I WAS NOTHING

I have to drive past your house every day on the way to work and *I hate it*. I turn up the music so loud I can't hear myself think. At least, that's the lie I tell myself. My mind is the loudest thing I know. Flashbacks of me laying my vulnerabilities down within its walls don't stop ripping shreds off my self-worth till I'm burying myself in meaningless distractions at work. The new owners have demolished the insides. Rubbish trucks carted it away limb by limb. It's been months now and it's (I'm) still empty.

I hate that I ever said yes to that first date. I hate that I felt anything at all. I hate that I gave another man another chance to abandon me. I hate my fragile heart. I hate that you have the same effect on inanimate buildings that you do on lovers. I hate that people now look at me the same way I look at that house.

Like it has been gutted.

Like there's nobody home.

Like the lights have been turned off.

~I hope somebody moves in soon

Some days I fear
all I'll know of love
is aching for hearts
that will
never be mine.

I keep telling myself
that *this*
is the crescendo
that your absence
cannot ring any louder
but the days drudge on
and it does.
It does.

- *I Miss You in Symphonies*

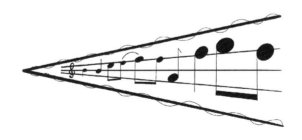

I keep searching
for love
in empty men

as if they hold closure

as if they'll answer me
in ways
you never would.

Am I enough now?
An I enough?

You may never have been mine
but I,
I was yours.

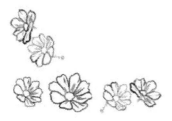

RAIN IS COMING

The fence palings look weathered today. Washed out. Grey. Like they've been nailed to a cross and exposed to the elements far too long. Algae grows in the spot our bodies used to press against, limbs intertwined and heavy in lust, laughing at the audacity of life and how we'd one day conquer it.

"Rain is coming," you remarked as we laid there catching our breath beneath a cornflower sky.

"There's barely a cloud in the sky?"

"It's coming," you insisted. "The ants never lie."

You were always so full of certitude. I had forgotten how much I missed that until I found an army of ants pouring in through the kitchen window yesterday morning marching seamlessly in one straight line along the stone bench.

Rain is coming.

I still hear your convictions in my head.

Maybe I mark off the calendar for the same reason addicts tally their days of sobriety. Regardless, I still count the days since I heard your voice and truth be told, it hasn't stopped raining since.

Forgive me
for taking back
my vulnerabilities
but I think
I'll keep them.

It's ironic
is it not?
That someone
so unworthy
of my words
could fill me
with them?

All I hear
is the absence
of your voice.

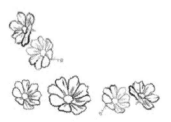

I LOVE SO HARD THAT I DON'T BEND, I BREAK.

I've spent years pulling myself apart, dissecting my heart, analyzing every relationship I've ever dipped my toes in searching for answers as to why I love as emphatically as I do. I arrive at no definitive answer other than life is a stairway of lessons I will never stop climbing; and the stairway back from hell is wall to wall with mirrors. There's no escaping your reflection. There's no denying the choices that led you there. I walk on shifting ground year after year and have grown to respect the way people walk into my life, tip it upside down and shake my world like a snow globe, splintering my self-worth into speckled white dots floating around me, settling on the ground, demanding I clean up the mess and make sense of what just happened, reminding me I am not nearly as bulletproof as I thought I was. We are supposed to come undone. Down there in the dirt with humility is where broken things rely on a strength beyond their own. There is a fine line between humility and ego. Both equally as important to the human condition. Ego protects us, elevates us, while humility grounds us, softens us. The truth is, despite what social movements may shout, we are not meant to endure this thing we call life alone. You can try but you won't get far. There's power in numbers and love can only be found in vulnerability. Humans are hardwired for connection and honestly, if you were to ask me what I treasure most I would say my relationships with those I hold dear. When I love someone-I mean truly love someone and I lose them. I don't bend, I break.

THE POWER OF LOVE

I rouse from a deep sleep to the sound of tiny water droplets tapping at my glass sliding door. *Pitter-patter, pitter-patter.* They sound like a group of giggling school girls asking to be let in. It is a welcomed distraction. I was dreaming of you again only to wake up smelling of loneliness. I swing my legs out of bed in an effort to shed the feeling of holding you and draw open the curtains. The moon is full tonight, pregnant with possibilities. I slide open the balcony doors and step outside. A gush of warm sea air hits my face, sweeping my hair behind my shoulders. Instinctively, I close my eyes, fill my lungs with the thick night air, and listen. Thunder rumbles off in the distance victoriously like a freight train charging through the clouds. The sky flashes neon blue and I am reminded that Mother Nature is the greatest of all artists.

The heavens demand reverence. Have you listened to the way everything falls silent when a storm rolls in? Even the sky's freedom riders plump up their feathers and retire to their nests. There's no denying God's power.

Solace paints itself across the aftermath. There, in the remorse of a raging sky emerges stillness. It's deceiving really. One could argue the gentle breeze played no part in tearing that seemingly indestructible tree in two. How could something so beautiful be so dangerous? We are bound by laws irrevocably decreed by nature. He that giveth can taketh away. Therein the face of love lies the power to destroy you.

It lingers doesn't it?
Like my perfume on your sheets.
You tell yourself you're happy
but can't forget the way
my eyes swallowed the stars
only to shine for you
that night twenty-six letters exploded
into salty streaks
down the sides of my face
she'll never look at you like I do.

"What are you looking at?"

"I'm just reading you," I smiled, admiring the way the fairy lights traced your side profile in the dark.

"Oh, is that so?" you laughed nervously as we weaved in and out of the crowd, fingers intertwined. "And what do you see?"

I never did tell you that you looked like Jupiter at twilight, forever burying my feelings beneath the way you held my hand like it was loose change.

I knew very well how foolish it was to fall for the first star to appear when it was only a matter of time before you filled another glass jar with coin-shaped memories you had no use for- till I became just another girl you used to know.

The last time we kissed I heard the penny drop and knew I'd spend the rest of my nights searching the sky for someone who shone as bright. I pressed my lips to your cheek and promised to stay safe. And when I said goodbye what I meant was *I'm sorry I was never enough.*

Just once I want to give myself to love
without being given back.

I REMEMBER THE LEAVING

I don't remember much before the leaving. There's a decade worth of calendar days I've wiped clean from my consciousness. Doctors tell me it's a means of survival~ that maybe it's best they stay submerged.

There's never any warning. My hands turn into earthquakes at the first sign of loss. Crimson needles pumping through my veins, my breathing quickens. I unravel. Not even the floor can catch me.

I don't remember much before the leaving.

I remember the sound of doors being ripped off hinges, daily. I remember smashed glass bottles, other women, hiding behind locked doors, children crying, meth eyes, the way he twitched in his sleep, a knife, the axe, flashing red and blue lights on the driveway. Police. I remember you holding a spray can, me hiding in a cupboard, the *clunk, clunk, clunk* of a metal ball ricocheting against the insides of aluminum tin. I remember crouching down and whispering, *"Let's play the game of who can be the quietest,"* to my four and five-year-old as we slipped out the front door, my newborn tucked in the shield of my right arm. I remember reading the words DADDY IS A MONSTER spray painted in red across the living room floor. I remember running. I remember never looking back.

I remember the ocean's sirens calling me for months before we left. The way I tasted sea salt before I sunk toes into its edge. Her sweet beckoning. The pull in my chest. The way I, through gritted teeth, tore marriage off my back like broken wings, sewed my shoulders back together, packed what was salvageable into a Daihatsu Terrios and drove towards to the sea with nothing but hope and my babies buckled into the backseat.

I remember the leaving.

I tried to cry out
for help
but there's nothing
more silent
than the scream
of a woman
under water.

Toss me to the wind,
I beg of you.
Set my heart free.

I have pockets of time mounted firmly to the back of my mind. There's fifteen seconds from grade eight drama class that hangs there defiantly.

I'm sitting cross-legged on the classroom floor, distracted by the colour of my socks- one was pink, the other blue with yellow stripes- I never could quite master the art of symmetry. I had wedged myself protectively between one of my best friends and a girl who kept smiling at him. I remember wrapping my arms around my ribs in a weak attempt to dull the ache, secretly despising myself for wishing he'd look at me the way he looked at her. Suddenly drawn back into the lesson, my hairbrained drama teacher starts twirling her hands theatrically quoting Shakespeare~

"All the world's a stage and all the men and women merely players."

As ridiculous as she appeared the unrequited lover in me never forgot that line, filing it in the back of my mind under 'self-preservation.' All these years later and I still am yet to master the art of finding matching socks or finding boys that look at me the way he looked at her.

A grown woman now, I catch my reflection in the rearview mirror and press the phone to my ear, momentarily seeking refuge in the way his voice hums melodically. He tells me all about his week and the loved ones in it and like clockwork my grade eight drama teacher starts twirling her hands theatrically quoting Shakespeare from the back of my mind~

"All the world's a stage and all the men and women merely players."

I wrap my left arm around my ribs protectively and take the stage. "I'm so happy for you," I reply convincingly. Shakespeare was right. We're all actors. Some more accomplished than others. He's never once heard the way my heart splinters every time he says her name.

Red Flags and Butterflies

You say my mouth is a trap door full of apologies and doubt and I say *I'm sorry*. Sorry the way you make me feel is fingers to a trigger. I am still learning that not all men's eyes are exit signs. I am sorry that love floods my veins with anxiety but when all you know is fight or flight red flags and butterflies all feel the same. I promise. I'll get it right.

I am sorry. Sorry I reach for you with one arm and shield my heart with the other; that I spend my days rewriting negative thoughts into sonnets and that July morning I couldn't tell you what was wrong my tears on your shirt were remnants of the past my mouth had forgotten how to speak.

If fear would loosen its grip on my throat I would speak of tender moments I can't quite shake. Those summer nights I slept in your arms and how the hum of your voice in a darkened room lit a match in my chest I'm still trying to put out. I would tell you of my dandelion heart and how it fights the urge to spill all my hopes and dreams in your hands, make a wish, and blow them away.

I would tell you how I'm jealous of the moon and how she climbs through your bedroom window night after night; that I watched her kiss your face as you slept, all childlike and innocent, and how it hurt to think of someone else waking up next to you; that your hand on my knee made my lips turn blue, that you make me hold my breath; that you smell like something impossible to forget.

But instead with trembling hands I say *I'm sorry*. You ask me if there's anything you can do and I ask you to hold my hand. What I mean is, I'm drowning in my mind. I mean, can you hold my head above water? I mean, it's taking everything I have just to remember how to breathe. I mean, give me a minute to loosen this grip on my throat and I promise, I'll get it right.

All The Things I Want To Tell You But Don't

- I spent the weekend packing my life into boxes.
- I'm sad you never got to see this house.
- I still pray for you every night.
- My phone barely rings anymore.
- There's a eucalyptus tree I park under every day that makes me wonder what you're doing.
- I miss the way you called me beautiful as if it were my name.
- I wonder if you read the book I sent you.
- I meant every word.
- Most days I'm okay. Others I'm not.
- I miss you most when I'm driving.
- I'm mad you never fought for me.
- I stopped counting the days I've gone without hearing your voice.

- I still don't know what I was to you.
- *I hate that you were my everything.*

What if I'm a language
no one speaks?
An anomaly;
a book left on a shelf.

What if this is it?

What if I'm never read?
What if I'm lost
in the only hands distance
allows to reach me?

What if I live out
my entire existence
staring love in the face
and never be seen.

"Where do you go when you go quiet?"

I thought of giving him a blanket response,
honeyed-lies, a branch of reassurance,
but a heart can only break so many times
and my tongue was thick with honesty.

"To the place where love dies."

I will kill us
so softly
you won't even hear
the gun cock.

I will go gently.

My last words,
velvet bullets.

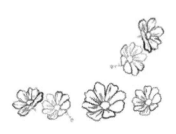

CHAPTER 3

Velvet Bullets

We broke like a family portrait
hits the floor.
All cracked smiles and shattered teeth.
You like to remind me I've changed
that I don't look so beautiful to you anymore.

This is what I look like when I don't love you.

If I'm guilty of anything
it's offering oceans to men
who wade ankle-deep in love
but are afraid to swim.

I have broke open
enough times to know
what I am made of.

Enough to know
I am too pure for this.

My intentions are like the waters of Puerto Williams I realized halfway through the conversation- too pure for this dating world. My voice cracked like eggs hitting the pavement.

"I'm just a girl who wants to be loved."

"I don't know what that means," you replied.

I cried myself to sleep that night, praying my tears might wash away the train tracks of anxiety looping through my mind. They didn't. I spent the next day avoiding eye contact and side-stepping conversation for fear someone might notice my shaking hands and ask the dreaded question- "Are you okay?" Amidst my obviate ploys, a group of little ones I taught last year came knocking on my classroom door.

"Miss!" They giggled, "Let us in!"

I squeezed the door ajar. "I'm sorry girls. I have a lot of work to do this break."

Unfazed by my request for solitude they pushed past me, bounding through the door. Clutching fistfuls of flowers and tugging at my wrists, they motioned me to sit on a tiny seat.

"Sit!" they demanded excitedly. Then with what one could only describe as benevolent tenor, they proceeded to fight over who loved me the most while kissing my cheeks and threading flowers through my hair.

"I love you the most," smiled one.

"No! I love you the most!" said another.

And as I sat there, tears streaming like drops of the Puerto Williams, I realized the love we so freely give does return home to us though, it comes from the only humans who can match it.

A Woman's World

I often wonder what a woman's world would look like?

Would we suppress our men? Would they fear what lurks behind street lights? Would men walk to their cars at night with keys wedged between knuckles? Would masculinity be seen as a weakness?

Would we pin them down and rip away what's not ours?

Would we objectify men as they walked down the street? View them as a possession? Tattoo pictures of naked men on our bodies? Would they check the mirror every time they left the house to make sure enough skin was covered? Would the poverty line be strung like a noose around the necks of fathers trying to raise motherless children?

Would men feel how I feel today? How it feels to be a woman?

Perhaps it is the human condition
that we love in ways we wish it to be returned.
Perhaps I am an anomaly.
Perhaps no one needs to be loved this emphatically.

That's the thing about depth.
It can be a lonely place.
You've got to come up for air
to reach most people.

I am letting you go
and you don't even notice
my palms subtle release.

Entangled through fingers
laces a whole new sense of foolishness.

I pretend it is nothing but know
it is the realization
you don't notice my fading hands
because you were never holding onto me,
at all.

I wonder if stars are just forgotten dreams,
hanging by a thread of hope,
aching to be remembered so they can fall.

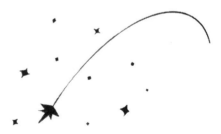

Never mistake a mermaid
for a girl
with shallow intentions.

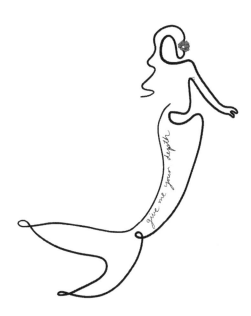

I will not love
all of you
and half of me
anymore.

I collected all the things
you robbed me of
and put them back on.

Strength
Love.
Innocence.
My maiden name.

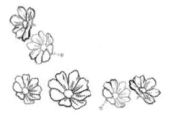

goodbye
(noun)

: the sound of everything
I ever gave you
returning back to me.

If our bruised insides
were as visible as
our polished outsides

would we handle
 one another with
a little more care?

Would our thoughts
be a little more gentle?

If I gave of myself
to everyone that asked
there would be *nothing*
of me left.

My worth
is not defined
by hands
that cannot
hold me.

First Day of Spring

I welcome the first day of spring the same way every year-
like an abandoned child, denude of all grace, leaping into
the arms of her mother.

"What took you so long?" I sigh, tearing open the curtains
to blink in daybreak, the full weight of my body crushed
against the glass. Thawing. I have always been this way,
though the more that time sinks in me, the more the winter
months sound like a leaky tap- taunting me- dripping to the
beat of perpetual longing.

Twelve thousand days on this planet and I cannot recite a
single one I have not ached for the sun. I sit by the window,
motionless, frowning at the way my fingerprints stain the
glass like question marks: 'Where am I meant to leave my
mark?' I never have carried answers to such questions only
a belly full of hummingbirds trying to migrate north.

The change of seasons always stirs them. Honestly, I don't
know what lies ahead. But I hear purpose calling me, and
it's higher than here.

135

I don't do well in crowded rooms.
I soak everyone in and become
more *them* than *me*,
having to go home
and wash it all away in a hot bath.
I always get dizzy when I stand up.
My mother once told me
it was because I let the water run too hot
but I think it's the sensation of my soul
rushing back into my body.

~ *Empath*

What does self-love look like?

The truth is I've no definitive answer but I can share a
story. I pried open my ribcage to make space for a timeless
little Italian seaside village today. I dragged my luggage up
and down miles of rugged terrain, climbed countless flights
of stone steps to get to my B&B. Exhausted, I swung open
the bedroom balcony doors only to be welcomed by
colorful terraces hugging the cliffs, overlooking the sea. I
took a sunset boat tour, laughed with women till my cheeks
hurt, fell in love with a language I could not understand, let
handsome strangers kiss my hand, tasted food I'd never
eaten and surrendered to the possibility of anything.
There's beauty to be found resting your feet in places no
one knows your name. When gifted the space to be
anybody you find a light switch to a room inside yourself
you never knew existed. I reflected on all the women I have
been torn into and grown out of over the span of my
existence and wished I could send them this moment in a
postcard, signed, *"It gets better."* And as the sun faded
tangerine and sunk beneath the sky, I found myself at home
away from home, on a boat, somewhere off the coast of the
Ligurian Sea and knew, if self-love could be painted in a
moment it would look like this.

You were never
brave enough
to bear my softness
and that says it all.

That says it all.

~ *Coward*

This person hurt you

I fold you in
like the top corner of a page,
an arrow,
a warning
anxiously pointing its tip
towards a chapter of my life
I promise to re-read
but never re-love.

CROSSES TO BEAR

There are days when not a piece of me is missing. Days
when fire burns beneath my breast and the blood of Joan of
Arc runs rampant through my veins. It is on these days I
believe you- those of you who nailed this cross to my back. I
hear the footsteps behind me of every person I've ever
known, reading my fate out loud-

Woman of Strength.

I shudder at the sound of it. There are days when the
responsibility of such a title weighs so greatly that shoulders
look like pillows and I wish for nothing more than
permission to sleep but pride will never allow it. Its grimy
fingers grip my throat till I straighten my spine and rid
myself of all weakness.

Strong is not a label I wear proudly rather what I became
when gifted no other choice. I will carry this cross. Hell, I'll
even smile while I do so, *but let it be known,*
I never asked for it.

I found peace
within
the absence
of you.

The curse of reaching a certain level of consciousness is that the world appears a hell of a lot less appetizing. I am a woman hungry for things I cannot find. Light is undeniable. In love. In career. In words. In rooms full of people. In intentions. I recognize it long before it speaks and I no longer possess any desire to exist where it is not. The problem with constantly listening for truth is going about life feeling all the spaces screaming its absence.

Do not mistake my lack of enthrall as emptiness. I keep the best of me under duress. Show me space that pulsates with truth. Grant me people I ache to unfold before. Give me something real and I'll pour so much of myself into it there won't be room enough to fit. Forgive me if I look like I'm disappearing. I only want for things that consume me or not at all.

BLUE LAKE

You told me God must have made my eyes from the waters of Blue Lake; that there wasn't a man alive who could not see to the bottom of them. Do you remember the day you laughed when I begged you to take me there?

"Let's go now!" I squealed, tossing crumpled bedsheets aside to jump on top of you.

"Now?"

"Yes, now! New Zealand is only a three hours plane ride."

"Lay back down and love me," you protested playfully, squeezing my waist between your thumb and forefinger.

That's how it always was with us. You, pining polaroids to the walls of my imagination. Me, fitting perfectly between your hands, folding like a napkin.

And I wonder if that's all you saw in my eyes from the start- two blue pools of pure intention, a safe place to swim, someone to love you through the oblivion.

A Beautiful Mess

If you're looking for perfection then keep walking. I'm a beautiful mess. I love more than self-preservation says I should and deal with the consequences later. I'm a slave to my senses and can't plan more than an hour ahead.

The only time I'll miss a sunset is to watch it set in your eyes. My hand will find a home in your back pocket and refuse to leave. I'm possessive. I'll kiss your cheek every time a girl walks past and hold your hand tighter than pride says I should. I choke on compliments and crawl through life on hands and knees. I build pedestals for others and have tattooed humility upon the soles of my feet.

I never wear matching socks and my hair refuses to be tamed. I'll warm my hands under your shirt and giggle when your nose wrinkles in disapproval. I'd rather make love than clean the house and my natural instinct is to run from confrontation. I'll buy take out instead of cook and dance around you defiantly in the kitchen to songs you hate.

I leave a trail of sand behind me everywhere I go and the ocean never stops calling my name. I'll kiss you when you're mad and turn you into poetry when you're sad. I'll sleep in your shirts and in my weakest moments I'll beg you tell me I am everything I fear I am not but I'll never have eyes for anyone but you.

If you're looking for perfection then keep walking.
I'm a beautiful mess.

I release you
like a
helium balloon
floating
higher and higher
knowing
all too well
you will never
come back.

Eventually the pain grows quiet.
Eventually you hear yourself again.

I can't sleep lately. I close my eyes as if with open arms but my body will not welcome rest. I've never felt anything lightly. Feelings explode inside me like fireworks I spend entire days walking around pretending I'm not feeling. A smile on my face. It is not a mask. I love everything about me with such rapture but I cannot deny the sadness. It is both a blessing and a curse to feel this deeply. I've always been this way. My mother thought me to be shy as a child but I was simply reserved. I still am. I don't give myself away lightly. To give myself away is to open flood gates few have the capacity to receive. There have been seasons I tried building a wall between myself and my feelings. They were months drenched in apathy. To close the door to pain is to close the door to joy, and when you've experienced joy at heights that feel like you're climbing a stairwell to heaven, you learn to bear the days of sorrow like a goddess in training because you know it is a gift to feel this deeply. You cannot embody one without becoming a vessel for the other. I discern light so knowingly it falls about me like the warmth of spring air. Like a language I was once fluent in; a memory that has been erased yet undeniably familiar; a compass leading me home I cannot deny. I was once asked, "How do I recognize what is good?" and I simply replied, "The same way I recognize the face of my father, I just know." I fumble my way through the darkness of this life guided by pillars of light. Searching for purpose. Searching for that ladder which leads me closer to heaven. Closer to home. Some days I find it. Others, I don't. Some days I sleep soundly. Others, my purpose haunts me. It never stops calling my name.

You only loved me when I was silent.
A pretty little thing with a mouth full of secrets.
You shouldn't feed a poet so many stories.
My clothes don't reek of pain anymore.
I plucked all the words you hung in the air
and put them on paper.

Your name does not
get caught on the way up
anymore.
No longer latches
to the walls
of my throat.

I am rid of you.

I lie to the man
behind the deli counter
and tell him I have a boyfriend
when he asks for my number
because if there's one thing
I've learnt in life it's that
men respect men's boundaries
more than they respect women's.

You think me
to be water.
A formless thing.
All ebb and flow
and gentle spaces.

And I am

but behind my eyes
I am all fire.

Have you ever seen
a house burn down?

I have.

Don't underestimate me.
I will burn your
whole damn world
to the ground.

do not mistake my kindness as weakness

A woman who knows her worth will dig a trench deeper than the Dead Sea between you and her in the seconds it takes you to pick your crown off the floor and put it back on. A Queen will worship the ground you walk on until you give her a reason that she should not.

Just a heads up, Kings. Woke women leave.

I cannot exist here.
I am a forever thing
and you've placed
an expiry date on me.

"You've changed," his tone was laced with cynicism.

I peered up at him. All six foot one of the man I used to break my back bending over backwards for. He balanced an all too familiar cigarette between his teeth, looking down on me through squinted eyes, taking another drag, searching my eyes for a slither of the person he used to know. I don't think I'd ever felt so tall.

"And you haven't changed at all."

You kept telling me
I was the only one
and I, desperate to feel
the weight of your love,
would pick up the words,
hold them to my ear,
and shake them.

They always sounded so hollow.

How many women
do you sing the same line to
at the same time?

Like the chorus of a song
in between the verses of us

"There's no one else"

I am such a hopeful thing,
dripping with maybes
and the spark of tomorrows.

The further we distance ourselves
from our mistakes,
the more at risk we become
of repeating them.

You cannot run from yourself.
The stairwell back from hell
is wall to wall with mirrors.

I outgrew you
like my favourite pair of shoes.
I still love them
they just no longer
fit me.

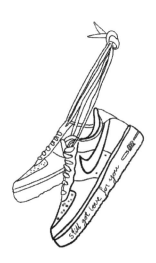

I hid my favorite pen underneath a stack of cleaning supplies on New Year's. We both know Stepford isn't in my vocabulary. I needed to forget what it felt like to love you. You never understood when I said '*love and words are the same thing*' until I stopped writing about you. I owed it to my ancestral line and every woman who ever died waiting on a man to forget.

It hasn't stopped raining in weeks and the roads are flooded. I watched a man drive through the rising sea level last night. He charged straight through in a black Ranger, *all unbothered,* water ricocheted off the tyres. I remembered how unhinged that made me. Me, rising. You, unaffected. Me, spilling out my skin. You, unbothered.

I don't need pills to get to sleep anymore and the ground stopped shifting. You were wrong. I didn't need a therapist. Turns out my trembling hands were the result of being dangled off a cliff and being told to wait.

I stopped waiting.

You think tenderness
to be my weakness
but I am yet to find a lover
who can stand with me in my power.

Unworthy opponents
they slink away defeated
unable to tame my unyielding softness.

I will not harden.
                I will not harden.
                                I will not harden.

The universe
does not speak
out of line.
That's your cue
to walk away.

I used to miss you.
Now I just remember you.

I was eighteen when I met you. White. Untouched. Bambi-eyed and naïve. Pupils like sponges thirsty for all colors of the world. I cannot remember how I fell in love with you but I read once humans dissolve memories as a means of survival. I found a note from 2002 where you call me an angel. Did you know white objects appear white because they reflect all colour and black objects cannot reflect light rather absorb all colour?

"You can't see the rainbow if you're not looking up," I'd say.

"We're different you and I," you'd reply pessimistically, lighter in hand, cigarette balancing between your teeth. I think maybe you did know. You just didn't count on me working out there was never going to be anything but darkness around you and you were always going to siphon what you could not give.

There has to be a place in this world
for a woman like me.
A place where fragility is not forsaken.
Where gentleness is a sign of strength.
Find me a home where love speaks softly
and meekness is sort out of the shadows.
Where hands are for holding.
Where tongues are not weapons and truth prevails.
Tell me, where do I belong in a world gone mad?
How does a whispering heart pierce all of this noise?

The past demands
to be felt.
Sometimes it runs
in simultaneous lines
down the sides
of my face.

Who am I
to deny a vessel
to that which
made me a warrior.

If I could tell my younger self anything it would be to think of yourself as a redwood tree. A beautifully unique redwood with roots so curious and thirsty they will dig deep searching for love. You are but a seedling now, full of innocence, beguiled by the sunlight streaming through the canopy above you.

As you blossom men will seek your beauty, reaching for your branches. You will mistake this for love. They will stunt your growth. Strip you of leaves. Strangle you with vines. Set you ablaze with love and diminish your sense of self to nothing but embers trodden beneath their feet on the forest floor. And it will rain. It will rain for so long you will wonder if you will ever see the sun again. You will. As you turn in and water yourself, sprigs of your former self will reappear and you will grow taller than you ever were, day by day, with ever-increasing wisdom. Slowly but surely, outgrowing every single tree that ever made you feel small; and you will look down and wonder why you gave so much power to someone so unworthy of your love.

You will spend many days wondering where he is-the one you are meant to share your life with. You will recognise him as someone who not only grows with you but intertwines his roots and supports your weakest of branches. You will bear one another up, weathering life's storms, and surrounded by all the beauty in this world he will only have eyes for you.

You see, you are destined to become so much more than you ever thought you could be and he will see you for the redwood that you are; and with arms stretched wide like branches his embrace will feel like a canopy of love that envelopes you and whispers, *"Never stop growing."*

I'm prone to indecision. It's a side effect of clutching caution with both hands. I haven't always held it this way. I've grown obsessively mindful of my time and just how valuable it (I) am. So mindful that I turn decisions over and over in my mind to the point of not making one at all.

Maybe it's the fear of failure or maybe I'm just trying to prevent myself from committing to another thing not meant for me. I torment myself by asking, "Is this a home for my hands?"

But sometimes, when I need it most, easiness falls about me and sweet moments whisper *you're where you're meant to be* and I let go of the past and the future and rest in the surety that right here, right now, there's no place I'd rather be.

And so I asked the universe,
"How do I feel all thing beautiful."

She smiled and replied, Open."

My aloneness unnerves the world;
labelled as an anomaly in need of fixing.
Tell me, just what is it you find the most unsettling?
That I feel whole without a man
or what I'll accomplish without one?

I will not
fall in line.
Conformity
is for the
walking dead.
Bind me with ropes.
I'll still sway.

Imagine a world
where people
spend less time
looking in mirrors
and more time
looking through windows.

Defences are heavy things
and I'm still searching
for a safe place
to lay mine down.

I am here
I am here
but it reeks of impermanence.

I hear whole life stories
in the hum of a voice.
I once heard a woman's voice break
when she spoke of her late husband.
As if her words fell down a crack in her throat
and couldn't get back up.

Growing content
does not feel like
growing at all.

It feels like settling
at the bottom of the ocean
telling myself
I do not want for air.

A sun haze dances in childlike streams through my bedroom window, kissing the bed of my cheek and through the blinking of eyelashes, temperance rouses me to a new day. The autumn wind is back, beating angrily against my side gate, reminding me another year has passed and I still haven't fixed the rusty latch or shook this perpetual state of restlessness. Mornings like these I wonder how I could be surrounded by so much familiarity yet still feel so lost.

My body has become a compass- north and south at constant war- hands reaching for higher purpose while my feet remain anchored to the floor. I lie to myself, say, *It's safer this way*. Only to find myself spitting out the bitter aftertaste of mediocrity. My head tells me I am blessed but my heart says hours are finite things, fading like fingerprints on lovers lost.

There are only so many nights I can lay across my driveway, bones heavy, counting the stars; midnight showers I can sink to the floor, head bowed, washing away the day. There are only so many mornings I can go on believing settling for this life is enough for me.

I know you are sorry
and I know this hurt
is no longer mine to carry.

I say it over and over
in the hope that one day I'll put it down
and believe the way remission sounds
falling from my mouth.

I forgive you. I forgive you. I forgive you.

A love like that shone so bright
I knew it would never die.
I could not keep you
so I added you to the stars in the sky
whom I love from afar
but cannot touch.

I think about how love appeared
from where you stood;
how it must have felt to watch someone
so unapologetically free,
and for a moment,
I'm not mad at you for letting me fall,
not even the tiniest bit,
not even at all.

Forgiveness

I stopped counting the circulations taken for the present to take hold of my hand but at last we stand in one place and as I bathe in this velvet light that is the end of the tunnel I can humbly testify I forgive you.

I think about it sometimes- the bloodied aftermath. Have you ever wondered why they say Rome wasn't built in a day but never speak of the destruction? The crumbling ruins of love. And by crumbling, I mean the grazed knees and trembling hands. I mean stolen air and gaping wounds. I mean the trodden I love you's and scarlet-letter-wrists. I mean the disintegration of oneself- lost in eternal darkness- void of all purpose.

I mean the 3 am's,

the 3 am's,

t h e 3 a m 's.

All that remains now is a monument. A ghost. Fear not, my love. I am but light now. It is true what they say, "There's life after death." Time has granted me breath again and I am so blissfully whole.

I no longer regret loving you like I did.

For if one day, heaven forbid, the cast iron cuffs of humility shackle themselves to your hands and your feet, and you're left to forge life in the same state you left me- alone- questioning everything you've ever known- counting dregs of self-worth like rusted coins found in the back pocket of old jeans, robbed of all pride, asking yourself why wasn't I enough?

Why wasn't I enough?

Why wasn't I enough?

You will be able to trace the lucid memory of a girl you once knew who invested every last drop of herself into the river of your eyes. And you will know that to one person in this world you were not just enough, but worth dying for.

I sunk into the ocean's mouth and let her swallow me whole this morning. Head tilted back, I laughed as the waves washed away my desire to be loved by you.

She crashed into me, pushed and pulled at my thighs, slapped me across the face, pressed salt into my wounds and severed the cord I had tied so completely to you. By the time she was done with me I was left with nothing but a raging sense of worth demanding to be honoured.

I forgave myself for every time I reached for you only for my arms to fall by my sides, heavied by the weight of nothingness; for every time I begged to know you loved me; for every time you shouted at me and I boarded up my windows, allowing myself to believe I was a broken home in need of fixing.

I do not need to be fixed.

I am whole.

My eyes- windows wide open. *My mind-* morning sunlight. *My lashes-* white curtains waving in the breeze. *My hips-* orchards plump with seasoned fruit- ripe for the picking. *My heart-* a labyrinth lined with lavender and gardenias. *My hands-* sweet peas climbing trellises. *My feet-* rock solid foundation. *My ribcage-* halls filled with laughter. *My lips-* cherry blossom trees. *My words-* the aroma of freshly baked bread drifting through the air. I forgive myself for all the times I tried to build a home in you and not me.

I release you to the sea. I forgive you. I forgive me.

Civil unrest between
the head and the heart
will not go gently into the night.

You can know your worth
and still fall for the wrong boy.
You can block his number
and still hope he calls.
You can never look back
and still be haunted by his ghost.

Forgive yourself for being utterly human.

Love is many things
and none of them are logical.

I'm so full now
I wonder if anyone
is strong enough
to hold me.

I lose myself in love.
I thought this to be my inherent weakness.
The way I know no other way of loving
other than building a home within its arms.
The way I melt into him like hot candle wax,
molding into the curve of his chest and navel.
The way my heart thumps-

stay   stay   stay

and never leaves.

But the right man will hold me there like an open door
with the road map back to myself
tattooed across his chest in permanent ink.
The right man will let me love him in the only way
I know how and lead me safely home.

You do not know me yet
but every night
I ask God the same thing.

"Please, be gentle with him till I find him."

About the Author

Cindy Cherie is a writer, poet, and teacher
from Bribie Island, Australia.

Find more of her work online:

Instagram: @cindycherie
TikTok: @cindycheriepoetry
cindycherie.com

Other books by Cindy Cherie

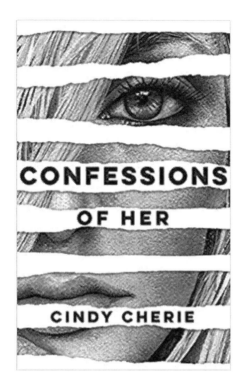

Confessions of Her is a tale of survival depicting how one young woman found love in herself, rather than searching for it in the arms of another. This autobiographical collection of poetry and prose takes the reader on a journey of love and loss, depicting how she overcame heartbreak to ultimately, save herself.

Fans of *Confessions of Her* are saying **"enrapturing"** **"I've never felt so seen"** **"emotionally charged"** and **"goosebumps for all!"**

Made in the USA
Las Vegas, NV
29 October 2021